Simple Machines
Wheels

Chris Oxlade

FRANKLIN WATTS
LONDON • SYDNEY

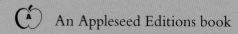 An Appleseed Editions book

First published in 2007 by Franklin Watts

Franklin Watts
338 Euston Road, London NW1 3BH

Franklin Watts Australia
Hachette Children's Books
Level 17/207 Kent St, Sydney, NSW 2000

© 2007 Appleseed Editions

Created by Appleseed Editions Ltd,
Well House, Friars Hill, Guestling,
East Sussex TN35 4ET

Designed by Helen James
Edited by Mary-Jane Wilkins
Artwork by Bill Donohoe

ISBN 978 0 7496 7570 7

Dewey Classification: 621.8

A CIP catalogue for this book is available from the British Library

Photo credits
page 5 Mathias Kulka/ Zefa/Corbis; 6 Chris Oxlade; 9 Chris Oxlade; 11 Rob & Sas/
Corbis; 12 Adam Woolfitt/Corbis; 15 Neil Rabinowitz/Corbis; 16 K & H Benser/Zefa/
Corbis; 18 Dietrich Rose/Zefa/Corbis; 19 Roger Ressmeyer/Corbis; 20 Chris Oxlade;
21 Alan Schein Photography/Corbis; 22 Gianni Dagli Orti/Corbis; 23 Chris Oxlade;
28 Dean Conger/Corbis

Printed in China

Franklin Watts is a division of Hachette Children's Books

Contents

What is a simple machine?

A simple machine is something that helps you to do a job. We use simple machines to help us every day. Here are some simple machines you might have at home.

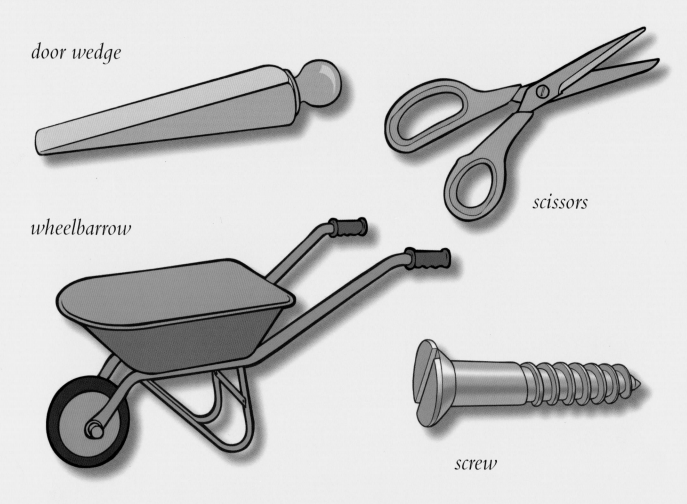

door wedge

scissors

wheelbarrow

screw

This book is about wheels, which are simple machines. The handle on a water valve is a wheel. Door knobs, tap handles and steering wheels are all wheels too.

This wheel makes it easy to open and close a valve.

Pushes and pulls

You push or pull on a wheel to make it work. When you push or pull, the wheel makes a push or a pull too. Scientists call all pushes and pulls forces.

A shower knob is a wheel. You push and pull to turn it round.

We show pushes and pulls with arrows. The arrow points in the direction the force is pushing or pulling. The longer the arrow the bigger the push or pull is.

This force arrow shows that the person's feet are pushing down on the ground.

Red arrows show pushes and pulls.

Blue arrows show movement.

To make a steering wheel turn, you push on one side and pull on the other.

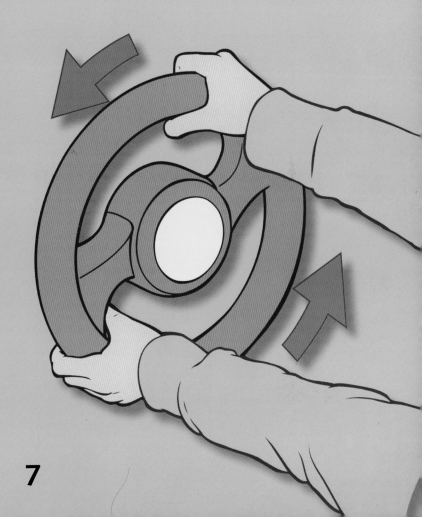

Making forces bigger

A wheel is a very simple machine. It is a disc of material, such as plastic or metal. A rod called an axle is fixed to the centre of the wheel.

This is a simple wheel and axle. When the wheel spins round, so does the axle.

A wheel and axle can make a push or pull bigger. You push or pull on the edge of a wheel to turn it. This makes the axle turn too. The turning axle makes a bigger push or pull.

This wheel is lifting a weight. A small pull on the wheel makes a large pull on the rope.

Helping things move

Wheels also make it easier for things to move.

If you try to drag something along, it rubs against the ground. This makes a pull called friction, so you find it hard to drag the object.

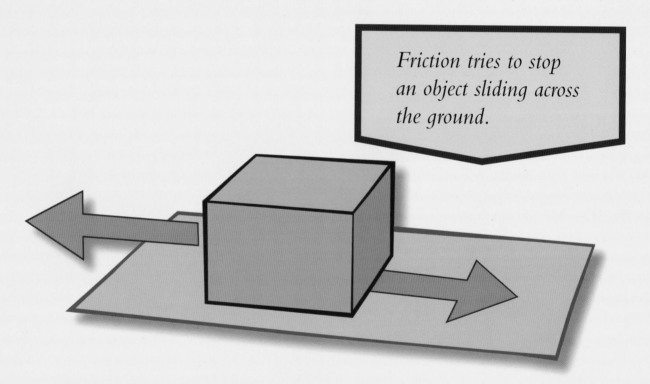

Friction tries to stop an object sliding across the ground.

Wheels help to reduce friction. They roll along the ground instead of sliding along. This gets rid of nearly all the friction. Wheels are attached to objects with an axle that can spin round.

Wheels let this boy push his friends along on their go-cart.

An object on wheels can be moved along with a small push or pull.

Turning with wheels

We use wheels and axles to turn parts of machines.

The axle does the turning. The wheel makes it easier to turn the axle. The handle of a water valve is a wheel. The axle works the valve.

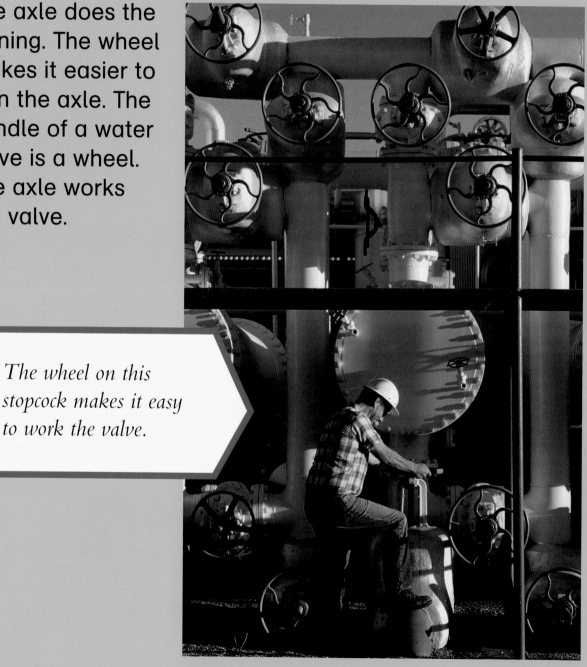

The wheel on this stopcock makes it easy to work the valve.

When you push on the wheel, the wheel pushes on the axle.

A door knob is a wheel and axle. The axle is a rod that goes into the door. When the rod turns, it makes the door latch move sideways. The door knob makes it easier to turn the rod.

When you twist a door knob, the door knob twists the rod with a larger force.

Steering with wheels

We use wheels to steer. A steering wheel makes it easier to turn a vehicle to the left or the right.

The steering wheel is connected to the vehicle's wheels. Pushing and pulling on opposite sides of the wheel turns the axle.

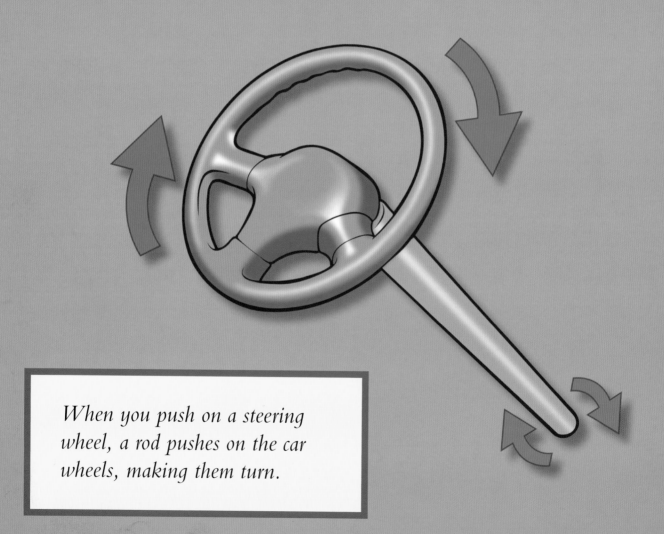

When you push on a steering wheel, a rod pushes on the car wheels, making them turn.

A large wheel makes it easy to steer a heavy yacht.

Large boats have wheels for steering too. A racing yacht has a very large wheel.

Pushing and pulling on the wheel turns the axle. This makes the yacht's rudder turn from side to side, which steers the yacht.

Gear wheels

A gear wheel has teeth around the outside.

When you put two gear wheels side by side, their teeth fit together. When one wheel turns, it makes the other wheel turn too.

These metal gear wheels are inside a machine.

Two gear wheels can make pushes and pulls larger. When a small wheel turns a large wheel, turning the small wheel makes a larger push in the large wheel.

When one wheel turns, it makes the other turn in the opposite direction.

When you turn the small wheel, it turns the large wheel.

Moving with wheels

We use wheels to move things along easily.

Skateboards, bicycles, trucks and trains all have wheels. The wheels are attached with axles.

Wheels let us move very heavy loads on trucks and trains.

The wheels on a scooter let you scoot along easily.

These parcels are moving along on a roller table. The table's wheels make it easy to push the parcels along.

Wheels in machines

Many machines use wheels to help them work.

Some machines have wheels that are turned by chains. The wheels have teeth around the outside that fit into slots in the chain.

A bicycle back wheel is moved by a chain. The pedals pull the chain and the chain pulls the back wheel round.

Pulley wheels change the direction of a pull on a rope, and can make pulls larger.

Cranes use pulley wheels to help lift heavy objects.

Some machines have gear wheels inside. The gear wheels change the push or pull from a motor, or make parts of the machine move faster or slower.

The hands of this watch are turned by gear wheels working together.

21

Wheels in the past

People have been using wheels for thousands of years.

The wheel is one of the most important inventions in history. It was invented about 6,000 years ago. Then it was used to make carts and chariots. Before then, loads were moved by animals, or dragged on sleds.

This carving shows a chariot made about 2,800 years ago.

These wheels scooped water from the river to pour on growing crops.

Engineers from Ancient Rome used gear wheels in mills for grinding corn to make flour. A water wheel turned one gear wheel. This gear wheel turned the mill stones.

Wheel fun

On the next four pages are some activities for you to do. They will help you to understand how wheels work.

MOVING WITH ROLLERS

You will need:

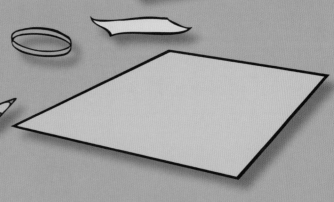

- a sheet of card (about 20 cm x 10 cm)
- some small books
- four round pencils or crayons
- a thin elastic band
- sticky tape

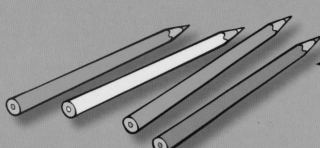

1 Attach the elastic band to one end of the card with sticky tape.

2 Put the card on a table top, and put some books on top of the card.

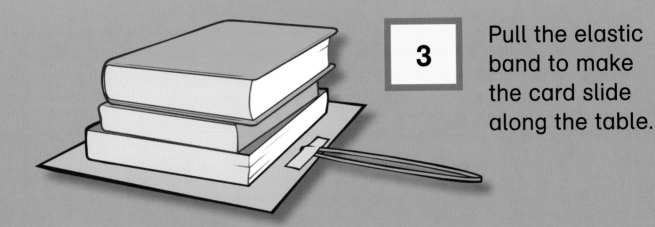

3 Pull the elastic band to make the card slide along the table.

4 Now put the pencils in a row under the card.

5 Pull the elastic band again to move the card.

The pencils work like wheels. They make it much easier to move the card and books. The elastic band stretches less because the pull you need is smaller.

LIFTING WITH A WHEEL

You will need:

- an old CD
- a old pencil or pen
- sticky tape
- 50 cm of string
- a small weight, such as a stapler or roll of sticky tape

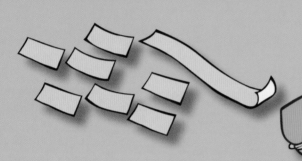

| 1 | Put the pencil or pen through the hole in the CD and tape it to both sides of the CD with plenty of sticky tape. |

| 2 | Tape one end of the string to the pencil near the CD. |

3 Tie or tape the weight to the other end of the string.

4 Rest one end of the pencil on the edge of a table.

5 Turn the pencil to wind up the string and lift the weight.

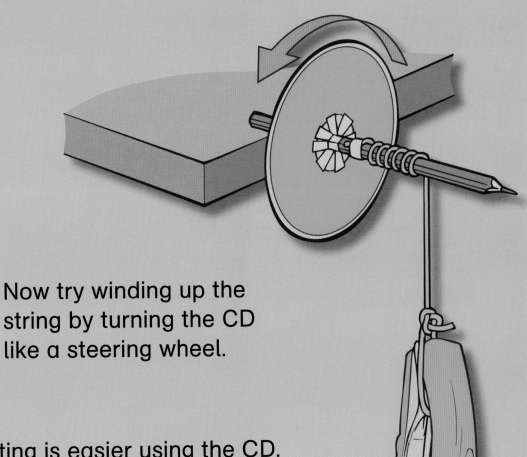

6 Now try winding up the string by turning the CD like a steering wheel.

Lifting is easier using the CD. The CD works like a wheel. It increases the pull on the string.

Spot the wheel

Can you spot all the wheels
on these pages? Try to work
out what each wheel does.

*This animal is turning
a wheel. What does
the wheel do?*

Where is the wheel in this picture? What makes the wheel turn?

Where are the wheels in this picture?

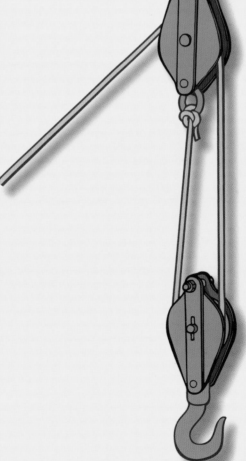

Answers are on page 32.

Words to remember

axle
A rod joined to the centre of a wheel.
The wheel turns the axle, or the axle
turns the wheel.

chain
A bendy metal loop made of many small pieces.
Teeth in gear wheels fit into holes in a chain.

gear wheel
A wheel with teeth around the edge.

forces
Pushes or pulls.

friction
A force that tries to stop things that are touching
from sliding past each other.

mill
A building where wheat is ground up by machines
to make flour.

rod
A long, thin piece of material.

roller table
A table with lots of rollers in the top.
Heavy things on the table move easily
over the rollers.

rudder
A flat piece of wood or plastic at the back
of a boat. It is used to steer the boat.

stopcock
A valve that stops water flowing along a pipe.

valve
A machine in a pipe that is turned
to open or block the pipe.

water wheel
A wheel that is turned
by flowing water.

Index

Answers to pages 28-29

The dark grey wheel is lifting water from a well to water crops.
The brown part is one large wheel. Falling water makes it turn.
It is called a water wheel.
This is a pulley system. The rope runs around wheels inside
the pulleys at the top and the bottom.